IF I MET AN ICE AGE ANIMAL

IF I GARDENED WITH A GIANT GROUND SLOTH

GRASSHOPPER

by Jenna Lee Gleisner
illustrated by Michelle Simpson

Tools for Parents & Teachers

Grasshopper Books enhance imagination and introduce the earliest readers to fiction with fun storylines and illustrations. The easy-to-read text supports early reading experiences with repetitive sentence patterns and sight words.

Before Reading

- Discuss the cover illustration. What do readers see?
- Look at the picture glossary together. Discuss the words.

Read the Book

- Read the book to the child, or have him or her read independently.
- "Walk" through the book and look at the illustrations. Who is the main character? What is happening in the story?

After Reading

- Prompt the child to think more. Ask: The main character imagines gardening and harvesting foods with a giant ground sloth. If an extinct animal could help you with something, what animal would it be? What would it help you do?

Grasshopper Books are published by Jump!
5357 Penn Avenue South
Minneapolis, MN 55419
www.jumplibrary.com

Library of Congress Cataloging-in-Publication Data

Names: Gleisner, Jenna Lee, author.
Simpson, Michelle (Illustrator), illustrator.
Title: If I gardened with a giant ground sloth /
by Jenna Lee Gleisner; illustrated by Michelle Simpson.
Description: Minneapolis, MN: Jump!, Inc., 2023.
Series: If I met an Ice Age animal | Includes index.
Audience: Ages 5-8.
Identifiers: LCCN 2021060798 (print)
LCCN 2021060799 (ebook)
ISBN 9781636909424 (hardcover)
ISBN 9781636909431 (paperback)
ISBN 9781636909448 (ebook)
Subjects: CYAC: Ground sloths–Fiction. | Sloths–Fiction.
Prehistoric animals–Fiction. | LCGFT: Picture books.
Classification: LCC PZ7.1.G5885 Ifc 2023 (print)
LCC PZ7.1.G5885 (ebook)
DDC [E]–dc23
LC record available at https://lccn.loc.gov/2021060798
LC ebook record available at https://lccn.loc.gov/2021060799

Editor: Eliza Leahy
Direction and Layout: Anna Peterson
Illustrator: Michelle Simpson

Printed in the United States of America at
Corporate Graphics in North Mankato, Minnesota.

Table of Contents

Digging and Harvesting

Today, Papa and I are planting the garden.

"I wish a giant ground sloth could help us," I say.

“Didn’t those go extinct more than 10,000 years ago?” Papa asks.

“They did!” I say.

“But if one was here today, it could use its claws to dig all the holes!” I say.

I start to think more about gardening with a giant ground sloth.

claw

Giant ground sloths lived during the Ice Age. Thick fur kept them warm.

But before the Ice Age, they lived in warm places. If I gardened with one, she could handle the heat.

Giant ground sloths were big! She could carry the gardening supplies.

They were tall, too. Giant ground sloths couldn't climb trees like today's sloths. But they could stand on their hind legs and reach high. Their wide tails helped them balance.

She helps me harvest fruit. She uses her claws to bring branches closer.

Her tongue helps her grab food, too. Giant ground sloths were herbivores. Teeth on the sides of her jaws help her chew plants.

tooth

She digs up weeds with her big claws. Then she eats them!

When the plants in the garden are fully grown, the giant ground sloth helps me harvest them.

She eats a lot of the food as we work. But she shares with me! Yum!

“It’s too bad giant ground sloths are extinct,” I say to Papa. “I guess we’ll have to garden on our own!”

Parts of a Giant Ground Sloth

Giant ground sloths stood up to 12 feet (3.6 meters) tall. They weighed up to 8,800 pounds (4,000 kilograms). Take a look at the parts of a giant ground sloth.

Picture Glossary

balance
To keep from tottering.

extinct
No longer found alive and known about only through fossils or history.

harvest
To gather plants and food from trees, gardens, or fields.

herbivores
Animals that eat plants.

hind
Back or rear.

Ice Age
A period of time, about 10,000 years ago, when a large part of Earth was covered with ice.

Index

To Learn More

FACT SURFER

Finding more information is as easy as 1, 2, 3.

1. Go to www.factsurfer.com
2. Enter "**ifIgardenedwithagiantgroundsloth**" into the search box.
3. Choose your book to see a list of websites.